Business Development for Professionals
How to Eat an Elephant – One Bite at a Time

William C. Johnson

Business Development for Professionals
How to Eat an Elephant – One Bite at a Time

Copyright © 2010 William C. Johnson

Design by Elisabeth Lull

All rights reserved. This includes the right to reproduce any portion of this book in any form.

CreateSpace

Nonfiction/Reference/Publishing

First Edition (November 2010)

ISBN:9781456359775

Contents

Introduction

Bite #1	Attitude Adjustment
Bite #2	Who?
Bite #3	Mental Models
Bite #4	Discovery
Bite #5	So What?
Bite #6	Features, Functions & Benefits
Bite #7	Invading Organizations
Bite #8	Networking-Schmoozing
Bite #9	Conferences
Bite #10	Reporting from the Front
Bite #11	Stories
Bite #12	Elevator Speeches
Bite #13	Qualification Process
Bite #14	Setting up Meetings
Bite #15	Preparing for Meetings
Bite #16	Meeting Goals
Bite #17	The Meeting
Bite #18	Follow Up
Bite #19	Constant Contact
Bite #20	Presentations
Bite #21	WebEx-Webinars-E-vitations
Bite #22	Be a Coach
Bite #23	Golf
Bite #24	Closing Philosophy

Introduction

You are a professional. You've spent years in school - grade school, high school, college and graduate school. Most, if not all, of you have a list of letters after your names signifying your accomplishments, and they are well deserved. After all of that, the last thing you want to be viewed as is a salesperson of any kind.

Having served my own time in higher education gaining a civil engineering degree, I understand what you feel and think about this role. This book is about changing preconceived notions you may have and replacing them with new ways of thinking about the whole sales and business development process.

I am going to start with the mindset that business development is somehow unprofessional or beneath your capabilities and work my way out from there, hopefully taking you along on a journey of self-realization and improvement along the way. Some of you may gravitate towards doing more business development; some of you may not.

This book contains useful concepts and ideas about developing and maintaining relationships that you will be able to utilize no matter where you go or what you are doing. I believe that you will find that what I am presenting is applicable to any professional services firm whether an engineering/architectural firm, a law firm or financial services. Professional services firms all have at

William C. Johnson

their core the foundational need to develop, grow and maintain relationships. This is the core premise for this book. I will use a number of anecdotes and stories to illustrate my points, and I will start with one right now just to get you into the swing of things.

A long time ago at the beginning of my career, I was out of work for an extended period of time with a young family and desperate to find a new position to provide for us. I applied for an outside sales position at Honeywell, Inc. They called it account management, but what they were really looking for were highly technical people who they could train in advanced sales and client development skills.

Two hundred fifty people applied for the position. I was fortunate to land the job, and it turned out to be a great one.

Honeywell was quite proud at the time (and probably still is) of their rigorous account management/sales training program. It was thirty days long and involved counselor-based sales training all day every day, and was heavily weighted toward effective interview and listening techniques. Each session was videotaped and then we all critiqued each other at the end of the day. It was extremely difficult at first, but very effective at modifying our behavior to match the model.

The trainer was a gentleman named Mike Thompson, and he was a consummate professional at training technical professionals. I remember the first thing that he said to us at the beginning of the whole training program. He said that he knew we were all professionals, most with degrees in engineering or other sciences, and that we might view selling with a somewhat jaundiced eye.

Then he said something that I will never forget, he said "Ladies and gentlemen, in this life you are always going to be 'selling' something to someone. An idea, a request to be on a team, a request to have something done for you....whatever, but it's sales and your choice is to either get good at it and become very successful at whatever you choose to do - or not." That was the end of the speech. Mike Thompson was right; we are all selling all the time. We are trying to convince others to adopt our ideas, do what we want them to do, or convince them to let us do what we want to do. Whatever it is that we are trying to be, convincing about is nothing other than "selling."

So the choice is yours -- do you want to get better at it? Do you want to learn how to be more convincing than your competition? Do you want to learn how to listen better so that you can help more? If you do, keep reading, and I'll try to arm you with specific tools and ideas that will support the advancement of your business development skills.

William C. Johnson

Bite #1
attitude adjustment

So I had this attitude toward selling, and maybe you do also, and we just can't seem to shake it. What are you to do? Change your attitude. But how, you say? Rather than seeing selling as telling or pushing your opinion on others, I needed, and you may also need, to start thinking of it as helping. You might think this change is just a simple turn of a phrase, but it really is not. It's a complete shift in mental models from thinking that you have to force something on someone else or try to overtly or covertly convince them of your particular value proposition, to figuring out what they honestly need and helping them with a variety of possible solutions.

If you can re-focus your attitude to understand that the end goal in business development is to help someone with issues and problems that they may have, then you will start to relax and the whole process will morph into something that is based on meeting someone else's needs, and this is a quantum shift. If helping is the goal and your attitude is to do well by doing good, what we need to do now is continue to go through this learning process a bite at a time-eating this elephant.

Story Time:

I represent a large engineering firm and we do a lot of work in the higher education market segment from coast to coast. In my travels, I met a gentleman who is in charge of design and construction for a major mid-Atlantic university. He is a great guy, very talented, on a campus on the move with lots of work we would like to help with, but with no immediate prospects. I'd met with him and discussed their campus and facility master plans and proposed various ideas on how we might be able to help with the process, but things just weren't meshing. He had great ideas to listen to and was just plain interesting and I enjoyed his company. I learned a great deal from him about a number of issues and struggles that people in his position have to deal with on a daily basis.

This type of information is great to develop context that can be used with interactions on other campuses. Learning from someone like this, who is being open and honest, is extremely valuable.

About five months later, I had the opportunity to take him and a few other people out to dinner at a conference in Pittsburgh, and we started to discuss various ideas for a one-day energy-focused event at their campus. He and I discussed what we as a firm could do to help to support this whole event. During the process of discussing the event, I had the chance to ask some questions about their energy situation on campus and give him constructive feedback and ideas for him to consider incorporating into his current planning process. We started planning the energy day, and we were subsequently invited to provide descriptive information on our firm for their announcements and to create and give a presentation; the relationship just continued to grow. About two months later, we received an RFP from an architectural firm for a master plan for his campus that included specific energy projects they were interested in accomplishing. There was a line in the RFP that was a verbatim quote from my previous conversations where I was just offering some, hopefully, helpful advice. The architect literally called and said "Do you see this particular line item?" and I said, "Well, yes, I do." He then said, "Does anyone else but you know what this means and how to do it?" and I said, "Well, I don't think so." Right after that we were put on the team and subsequently received the work, completed this project and were invited to expand our scope of services on campus.

At the beginning of the relationship, I was just helping and had no idea where it might lead. It took eight months. Our firm will, we hope, be on this campus for a long time providing a variety of services. It's all about relationships and helping, which is what I was focused on while I went through this time period. If you keep your eyes on those two fundamentals, everything else will fall into place.

William C. Johnson

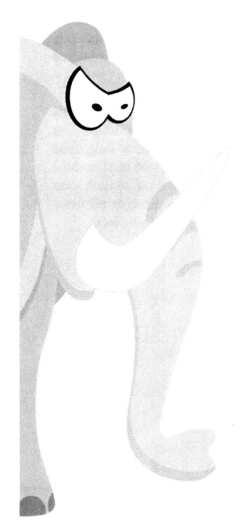

Bite #2
Who?

Who should be doing your business development? Remember, it's not marketing; it's business development. Marketing is designed to provide ground cover for business development. Marketing is proposals, print ads, public relations information, webpage design and everything that revolves around branding. It is categorically not business development. So, who should be doing business development, and what are the characteristics you should be looking for – either in yourself or someone you're going to start to mold for this important role?

Malcolm Gladwell's book "The Tipping Point" identifies two distinct business personalities. We have the "connector" and the "maven". A connector is someone who gets a great deal of personal and professional satisfaction from connecting people to one another for their mutual benefit. This type of person is all about helping others and always on the lookout in the back of his mind, listening to conversations for any hidden needs that he might be able to help with, either directly or indirectly, through his extensive and varied network. He has a database full of useful names that he has developed over the years always at the ready. He really doesn't have ulterior motives; he absolutely loves to connect people with other people so that needs are met.

A business development professional must be friendly, positive, inquisitive, quick on their feet, and bullet-proof. By bullet-proof I mean that they don't take rejection personally when they're out in the marketplace. Being inquisitive is extremely important because genuine interest in others shows respect and caring, and the most powerful way this characteristic is exhibited is through thoughtful questions and by active listening. Thoughtful questions open up a whole different dimension of communication that most people don't take the time to practice or concentrate on. Listening is such a powerful tool in the toolbox!

We have two ears and one mouth for a reason. We should be listening twice as much as we're speaking. Listening is far more powerful than speaking in that it projects caring, empathy and – most importantly – respect. I have found over the years that a respectful attitude in the face of circumstances that didn't deserve it has served me well.

There have been plenty of occasions where I really wanted to say something because of a barb aimed my way, but haven't. Without respect, nothing of value ever gets done. So the person who is interested in moving into business development must be capable of actively listening for all the right reasons.

If you're in business development you must be able to think rather quickly because opportunities can present themselves in so many ways it's really hard to list the variety. You need to be able to engage people in conversation and be comfortable doing so.

Being an extrovert helps, but isn't required. I've known seemingly introverted people who are extremely effective business developers because of the passion they have for what they represent. They are able to compensate for their personal discomfort by being prepared with a line of questions prior to any meeting and through just plain, old-fashioned practice.

Being friendly might seem to be obvious, but it's not. I've known some very senior people in professional firms who were not very friendly at all, and when they tried to develop relationships they failed to do so because their attempts were seen through as being shallow and self-serving. It comes across pretty quickly if someone isn't ready to really invest in relationships.

You will already know if you are inquisitive, quick, and friendly – but are you bullet-proof? What does being bullet-proof look like out there? If you are going to be in business development, you need to be bronze on one side and flesh and blood on the other.

I used this description one day when someone asked me how I was able to stand the constant rejection involved in making countless phone calls and sending innumerable emails during normal business development activities. I explained that I was bronze on the side facing the process and all the negatives and opposition, but that I was flesh and blood on the side facing my team.

You have to be able to absorb a tremendous amount of negative attitude and not react to it or let it get you down. We all have bad days. When I have them I usually take someone I really like to lunch or go play golf. It's a much better use of time to get re-adjusted rather than fume.

I have always been impressed with people who thoughtfully respond rather than react to situations. They calmly consider what to do in the midst of great turmoil and then respond in an appropriate manner. Usually this type of response completely baffles about 90 percent of the people around them: they're so used to seeing people react instantly and emotionally that they don't know what to do with someone who thinks before reacting. This ability to manage their reaction has the strategic advantage of placing the person who can do this in control of the situation. Exercise control of yourself and you will wind up controlling entire situations. Control is where you want to be in business development. The most accomplished business development people craft a defusing response when they are aggressively challenged or attacked. It reminds me of a member of the bomb squad calmly evaluating a situation prior to acting. These men and women do not go rushing about and start to rip wires off the explosive; instead, they are deliberate in their actions to defuse the bomb.

We need to practice the same deliberate approach. Remember, some people will either lob bombs your way on purpose or subconsciously just to see if you can stand the heat. If you can pass the test, sometimes these people will become your best supporters. Being able to defuse situations is a rare talent and takes great humility, love and patience.

Story Time:

I met a very accomplished Ivy League school campus architect. He was very bright, a little brash, and not a little talkative. The first time I met him, I couldn't get a word in edgewise, so I didn't try. I eventually had the chance to ply him with a few questions, and kept him going and he went on non-stop for at least an hour. At the end of this conversation, he finally noticed that I was still listening and asking questions and engaged. He saw that I wasn't going away, and he couldn't drive me away. I actually found him quite engaging, very bright, and extremely good at what he did. After a bit, I figured out that he really did have a strong grasp for the subjects we were discussing and had a lot to offer. His demeanor would have put most people off, but I don't give up easily. For the rest of the conference, two more days, he stuck to me like glue. It was amusing at one point because he'd be with me when someone new would come into my orbit, and I'd be explaining what we as a firm did and would be asking questions of the person and engaging them. At the end of one such conversation, he said, "You certainly have a unique way of going about this; all you do is ask questions, and you don't offer information unless really asked." He got it, and we are still continuing our conversations and have recently begun to work on his campus, helping them with a variety of issues that we uncovered while I was listening during our preliminary conversations. I don't think many people have run the gauntlet that he sets up. It's like his personal qualification process.

You have to be ready to adapt to situations like this one if you are going to be successful. Remember, respond thoughtfully, don't react impulsively, even when you want to and would be justified in doing so. It will not serve any useful purpose.

Business Development for Professionals

Bite #3
Mental Models

We all have them. Some of them are cultural, and some of them are learned from our contemporaries and peers, but we all have them, and they impact our perception of ourselves and others. They are like filters that give our world a particular shade and hue that's unique to our experiences.

Here is a list of potential mental model candidates that you may have encountered from time to time. Maybe I'm putting some words to a thought you've had in the past, but the important thing is to recognize them and their potential impact on your effectiveness at growing new relationships and your business. I will try to debunk them as I go. You may or may not agree with my thoughts on them, but at least consider what I'm saying.

- *All we sell is time* – This one is classic, and if you want whatever you do to be viewed as a commodity or to be commoditized, this one will do it quite nicely. When firms have this attitude ruling their business development structure, they are in a race to the bottom. We'll discuss racing to the top later on. The death spiral of commoditization, where all you are selling is time, puts you in the position of just another vendor. What needs to happen here is a major "re-think" on the unique value proposition you are really bringing to the clients you serve.

- *Faster-Better-Cheaper* – Is this really what you're after in growing your business, rather than moving to a trusted advisor, high-value-added, benefit-driven partner with your clients? This model is closely related to "all we sell is time!" I'm not saying we shouldn't be wringing the waste out of what we do and adding greater value to our work products. But consider that better-faster-more valuable might be better in the long run.

- ***The Billable Ratios Rule*** – If you want to put the final nail in the coffin of business development, continue with this one, and nothing will get done until no one has anything else to do and you're scrambling for work. What falls out of this one is the common refrain that you're too busy with "billable" work to pay any attention to business development and that when you are less busy you'll make some calls and see if you can stir up some business…you'll go "marketing." I've heard this one from so many people that it makes me nuts. I am going to give you a truism right now, and I want you to write it down and memorize it. *People do business with people they like.* Now, I want you to ask yourself a question. Who likes someone who only calls or contacts them when they need something? No one that I know.

Sporadic business development that is driven by the billable ratio bogey man is no business development.

If you don't want to do business development, then hire a professional who can be 100 percent externally focused and support them in all their activities in client relationship development.

If you disagree with this approach just think of the cyclical nature of how work gets done in a firm full of seller-doers. Everyone goes out when things are at the bottom of the curve and lands a whole boatload of work. Then they get busy doing all the work and maybe even have to expand the staff to do so. Then the work runs out, and they say, "Oh my gosh! Have the staff go and find a whole pile of new work!" This up-and-down method wreaks havoc on the financials of the firm and puts all kinds of pressure on everyone pretty much all of the time.

I'd ask you to consider a different model: the BD/seller in conjunction with the closer/doer model. The old seller/doer turns into the closer/doer and the firm hires a BD/seller to constantly prime the pump. This concept flattens out all those high-amplitude financial sine waves on your income statement and will set the y-axis well above break even! Billable ratios, in my mind, are headed for the dustbin of engineering management history if client satisfaction and value-driven companies are our future.

- ***The Commodity Cop-Out*** – We're "commoditized," you are saying, and you consider this the end of the world. Well, do something positive about it. Develop a new strategy and new services and – possibly – a new look that will effectively differentiate your firm. You need to clearly define and understand your unique value proposition. Get your team in a room with a trained facilitator and some of your best clients to really go at the whole value equation of why they work with you. By hiring a professional facilitator you can make sure that everyone is engaged and part of the process.

One of the keys to this type of process is to not jump to solutions prior to identifying your shared values and your shared vision. When they are clear to everyone, then you are ready to proceed with developing solutions. Don't ever forget that "all of you are smarter than any one of you."

Closely aligned with the attitude that you have been commoditized is the frequently used refrain, "we're too expensive." Have you ever heard that one? It's usually said with a defeatist attitude in the voice. This admission is stated like it's the end of the firm.

The company that I work for offers very high quality services and this comes at a cost due to the expertise and experience of our staff. We take a great deal of time and have carefully developed our value proposition and have articulated this in a variety of ways so that our clients truly understand the value we are bringing to the table.

When I was with Honeywell years ago, we were consistently more expensive than all our competitors but because of the superior service and equipment we provided I actually found that the price factor didn't impact my effectiveness. People now will tell me

William C. Johnson

"Boy, you guys are pretty pricey on this environmental work"…and my (thoughtful) response sometimes is, "We're cheaper than the lawyers will be if this job doesn't get done properly!" You get what you pay for. Ask yourself a question here. Why do people buy Volvos? Are they the cheapest? Are they the fastest? The answer to both of those is NO. What they are is one of the safest brands on the road, and, because they are, people are willing to pay a premium.

Are you the safe choice for your clients? Are you the ones they turn to when they think of reduced risk and improved service? If you aren't, why not? What is it going to take from you and your team to clearly point out the true value that you bring to your clients so that they can see it? How are you going to position yourselves so that you are taking full advantage of the value you bring? Take that Volvo picture, tape it to the wall and apply it to your offerings…see what pops out.

- ***"Our Clients/Propects Don't Understand Value"*** – And what are you going to do about changing this perspective? How much time are you spending with your existing clients and new prospects carefully educating them regarding your services in conjunction with your interviews with them? If people don't understand the value you are bringing, then it's probably because you don't understand it clearly either and, therefore, haven't clearly articulated your value to them.

Remember, people are going to do business with you based upon their perception of the benefits associated with doing so; that's where the value is, in the benefits and meeting their expectations of those benefits – not the features and functions.

Take a close look at your literature and your website. Do they resemble your competitors' to the point that you could just change your name and nothing else would need to be adjusted? I'm not kidding; try it! Go to all your competitors websites and look at what they are really saying about themselves and then what you have on your page or in your marketing literature. What do you see? Could you really just change the names? If so, you have a problem and the first firm that takes the time and exerts the effort to figure it out wins.

- *Telling is Selling* – Telling is not selling, it's actually anti-selling. As we've already covered, selling is all about helping, and, if helping is the motivating attitude that's directing you, you've crossed the Rubicon into sustainable business development.

    Believing that telling is selling is a prescription for disaster for the professional.

It's why professionals think that they hate selling, because they find it uncomfortable to be seen as being self-promoting and or viewed as forcing their opinions on others. So don't do it. And, what's more, don't let anyone else in your firm do it either.

When professionals understand that the discovery process is the heart of real business development, everything about their attitude and approach to business development can change. They begin to see the business development process in a whole different light, that of understanding through thoughtful questioning and discovery of the needs, values and goals of the other person. When professionals grasp this perspective, they can more effectively develop the skills and talents necessary to be successful.

Application:

Take some time and interview some people in your office with the goal of uncovering why you do things the way you do them. Pick a process, any process, and ask why you do it that way. You may have to ask it multiple times to really get to the core of the understanding, but eventually you will uncover mental models that are the foundation for the behavior. After you've uncovered the mental models, really hold them up to the light and see if they are valid. You will be amazed at what you may find.

Business Development for Professionals

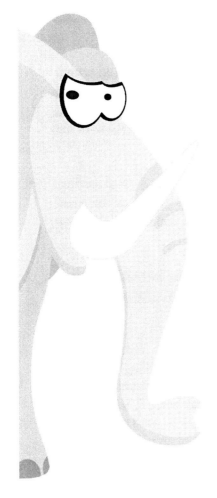

Bite #4
Discovery

Most people who try to sell, I mean really <u>try</u> to sell, fall into a category that I like to describe with the phrase "showing up and throwing up," which is what most people do when they try way too hard. They come roaring into the office of a prospect with their own set agenda and "throw up" all over the place. I may be exaggerating here, but I want to emphasize do not do this, and, if you have done it before, stop, and, if you're thinking of doing it take a vow of silence, forever!

You are a professional, and for years you have been taught the most powerful tool in business development. I guarantee that you are expert with this tool. You know it. You wield it with grace and expertise. It's the tool with the label "discovery process."

You have been taught how to do legal, engineering, business and financial fact finding by asking a thousand pointed questions with a couple of hundred follow-up questions just for good measure.

I want you to hear this and really listen carefully. <u>I want you to follow the same process exactly…*but change the questions.*</u>

Change the questions of discovery to focus on the prospects' needs, wants, perceptions, goals, fears and perceived benefits. Believe me when I tell you that you know how to do this, and believe me when I tell you that showing up and asking questions is a lot easier, more comfortable and about a thousand times more effective than "throwing up." Later on we will discuss questions and spend some time with interview techniques, but I wanted to make this concept absolutely clear to you early on so that you can consider it as you go through the rest of this book.

You are a trained professional. You have been trained to be inquisitive and insightful. You do not need to be an orator if you aren't talking. People will tell themselves that they don't speak well in front of others. If this is the case, then don't. Ask questions and listen. Remember what I said previously -- you have two ears and one mouth for a good reason.

Here's a little game you can play, it's actually kind of amusing. The next time you meet someone at one of the countless dinners we all attend or one of those early morning meet-and-greets, try this as an exercise. When someone introduces themselves to you, just give them your name and your company and get the first question in, the who, what, when, how questions. Keep them open-ended and keep questioning them about what they do, for whom, what cool projects are they working on, keep it going for as long as you can. Eventually they will turn to you and say something like, "What kind of business are you in anyway?" By that time, you should have a pre-manufactured answer based on all the information that they just spent the past five minutes giving you. It should be custom tailored just for them and aimed directly at what they might find most intriguing.

Try it; it is good practice for later on, when you are in front of someone's desk doing exactly the same thing. Practicing in this manner will make you expert in fairly short order, and by using these breakfast/dinner forums as a place to rehearse, you will get double duty out of them.

Application:

1) Come up with five or six questions that you are always going to have at the ready.
2) Practice them on people in the office
3) Take note of the responses and how long you can keep the conversation going by just asking questions.

Business Development for Professionals

Bite #5
So What?

William C. Johnson

What do I mean, "so what?" Here's the picture I want you to imagine. You're at a preliminary meeting with a new prospect, and you are on a roll describing all the cool stuff your firm does, all the great services you have to offer, all the incredible expertise you have to solve their problems, all the amazing clients that you've worked for, and all the gigantic projects you've done on time and on budget. You are in high gear, and your listener is going glassy-eyed on you. So you try harder, speak faster, louder with more energy, but the glassy eyes are getting worse. Pretty soon you half expect a thud as their head hits the desk. What's up with that?

I'll tell you what's up: you are forgetting another fundamental. Imagine that everyone you meet when you are presenting an idea or proposal has a 3 by 5 index card taped to their forehead with the question "So What?" printed on it, because that's exactly what they are thinking in the back of their minds. They probably won't say that out loud, but subliminally they are asking, "What does this mean to me; where's the value in this?"

This happens with great regularity because most people are very comfortable discussing in great detail features and functions of what they do or have to offer, but are generally unaware that they need to make the conscious connection to an actual benefit that the client can recognize. This flaw is fundamental in most presentations, talks, interviews or panels, and it is the reason that professionals involved in business development **need** the image of the 3 by 5 card taped to their audience's forehead. People need help making this connection between features/functions and benefits, and it's your job to do so early in the conversation.

The key is that you need to determine first of all what they value (by listening), what's the benefit that they are seeking, what floats their boat, what's keeping them up at night, what do they want, or what do they really need that they can't find. These needs can only be determined by carefully thought-out questions and interview techniques that we will discuss later on.

Remember that people are really looking for the benefits, not lists of services, features and functions. The benefit of owning a Volvo is that when the tractor trailer runs that red light, you're walking away; that's value, that's what you bought, not the sixteen airbags and the stainless steel roll cage capable of taking a direct hit from a 3-megaton atomic bomb. You don't care about that detailed list of features. You just want to know that you get to walk away from the crash.

Story Time:

Now for a story to illustrate. A firm that I worked for wasn't the least expensive on the block but they were definitely the "smart kids," which is what I affectionately called them. (Just as a side note: if you have a choice about who to work for, choose to work with the smart kids…even if they are pricey.) So, I found myself at a conference, and I was listening to someone describe their latest project that was in the planning stages. I was asked what we could do to assist and gave them an idea of the kind of value we could bring to the process. Instead of pulling out a company brochure or reciting the company mission/vision statement, all things that could have been done, I told a story to illustrate our value.

We had a major healthcare project in Maine, where a medical building had been sited on a very challenging piece of property due to extremely poor ground conditions. The original foundation design had called for the building to be on piles, which were very expensive and time-consuming to install. After we'd had a chance to thoroughly evaluate options, we asked if the space could be re-programmed and a single below-grade basement floor could be created where the mechanical equipment could be placed. This design approach would have the effect of unloading the site by the removal of the unsuitable soil overburden, allowing use of a mat foundation, eliminating the need for piles and saving $750,000, or about six times our fee. The architect and the owner agreed, and the basement was constructed. The savings realized were put back into additional features in the above-grade space where it could be truly appreciated and <u>valued</u>.

Cool story and true, and it certainly showed the value we brought to the project and really got the prospect's attention. The planner who was working with the facility as an owner's representative subsequently hired us for a series of projects. This story was designed to start with the features and functions and end with a large benefit that illustrated our value.

Start thinking of stories of your own that truly illustrate the value that you bring to your clients. We will be talking more about stories and how to use them later.

Meanwhile, when you're having your next strategic conversation with a new prospect (or even an old client), remember the file card taped to her/his head, asking that age-old question, "So What?"

Application:

1) Take some time and really read your company brochures and take a look at your web pages, and every time a feature or function is mentioned see if there is a corresponding benefit anywhere to be found in the same sentence. This review can be a sobering exercise. Now take more time and re-write those sentences to include the associated client benefit; be subtle, but get them in there.
2) We will discuss stories in a while, but you want to have a couple of them ready for use at any time, so think of them ahead of time and go over them… or go ask some people that you work with about some that fit a variety of situations and are clearly aimed at answering the question "so what?"

William C. Johnson

Bite #6
Features, Functions, and Benefits

Clearly explaining the features and functions of what you do and why you do it and what this means to the client is fundamentally important to the business development process. I know that I've been discussing benefits and their importance in the process, but it really is a three-legged stool; they are all required to fully explain your value, but they must be kept in balance. Features are the "what you do" and functions follow as "why you do it" or "how you do it."

In professional services there are a myriad of tasks that we perform for our clients that are important in meeting their needs or goals. They need to know that we can expertly perform these functions based on the experience and expertise of our staff and management. They may already have a list of tangible and, possibly, intangible benefits lined up in their minds of why your services are of direct benefit to them, but it is equally probable that they may not. You won't know what's driving or motivating them until you ask. You could assume that they would perceive the standard benefits of a particular feature based on their industry. But they may have other underlying needs and benefits associated with that particular feature that can be very beneficial for you to flush out.

It's also possible that they don't really understand the connections between what you offer and the value that they are seeking through your involvement. Remember, this is a bit of a contest between you and your competitors, and the firm that goes through the discovery process most thoroughly is probably the one that will establish the long-term relationship.

Figuring out what is really motivating the client can be extremely effective in building relationships and trust, which are at the core of most client decisions in hiring consultants.

With this in mind, you might want to start a line of questioning that is aimed at determining exactly what they are trying to accomplish, how they'd planned for it in the past, what the results were (maybe that's why you're in the room), and what the major tasks are they think need to be accomplished to meet their goals. This conversation is not meant to be a specific scoping discussion, but it certainly will put some meat on those bones; it's meant to get a clear understanding of what the client thinks they need and how to get there so that you can see the gaps in their experience or thinking, which is where you are going to help. We will discuss interviewing later on, because it is one of the most important skills for you to hone.

Story Time:

This story is about one that got away. I had developed a nice relationship with a large institutional prospect and was in the process of asking questions and truth-testing various services that we could provide for an upcoming expansion project. I had done this by sharing information, calling, playing golf (also the subject of an upcoming bite), and generally staying in touch at strategic points in their planning process. I created interest in a particular offering of ours that seemed to have significant traction. The prospect expressed interest and understanding regarding what I was proposing, and we had a couple of lengthy telephone conversations regarding exactly what they might like to do and how to structure the program to carry it out.

My contact shared planning documents with us, and we prepared a customized proposal for them delineating what we were going to do and how we were going to go about it. Somehow in all the conversations that I had with this prospect, I didn't fully grasp two things, even though I asked specifically about them.

One was how the decision making process was actually going to work. Secondly, I should have gotten more definition on their economic model and expected qualifications and so on. Price was far more important than they initially indicated, as was the ability to serve what they termed "one stop shopping" for an expanded scope that wasn't even in the RFP, nor discussed in my earlier conversations.

Unfortunately, prospects have the prerogative to change the playing field on you. Even with the best and most exhaustive interviews and meetings, you can sometimes be blind-sided by unforeseen circumstances. There are two lessons here: one is that they can change their minds and, two, it's never over. They did sign a contract for the work but the grant funding that they expected didn't come through, and the technology on our end has advanced and the this has left the door open for another opportunity.

There is actually a third lesson and that's to keep the door open. Even after we lost the initial opportunity I stayed in the conversation with this prospect, maintained the relationship that I'd started and because I did this we positioned ourselves if the project comes back to life. Never give up!

Business Development for Professionals

Bite #7
Invading Organizations

You are out there mixing it up with your clients, asking a zillion questions, learning all sorts of amazing things about their companies such as how they do business and what they need. During the course of conversations, they mention some organizations and associations to which they belong (and if they don't you should be asking!). And you've heard of these same associations from other clients and prospects on more than one occasion.

It's time to investigate whether it's worth your effort to invade. Invasions need plans. There are a couple of questions you need to ask yourself at this point about what your plan may look like. Are there more clients I'd like to work for who are involved with these particular organizations? Are there strategic team members who might work for my client groups attending these meetings and could they help my business? Are there specific learning or visibility opportunities available? Are there opportunities to get involved on a committee? Is it well run? Can I at least see a remote possibility of being on the board?

You need to vet the organization thoroughly, and, if it passes the test and it's populated by a number of potential clients, you might want to invade. But understand this -- it's a process, and the key to successful invasion is pretty simple. All you have to do is show up all the time. Ninety percent of your success with this strategy is in showing up and being seen, becoming part of the fabric and a quantity known to be involved. If you aren't willing or don't have the time to invest in the invasion, don't waste it on this endeavor because your results will be less than satisfactory. Some people go to meetings periodically and say what a great time they had and that they were out "marketing" or doing "BD," but they really weren't.

Socializing is important, but with organizations there has to be a real long-term purpose to this activity. You really need to be able to trace work back to these relationship building networks. It may take time to do this, but you at least need to see the possibilities building through your involvement that work will come.

Here's what I do once I've located an organization that I am going to try on for size. Naturally you do your research either on line or through your friends, and that's nice background, but what I do is call the executive director or an area VP or someone in the hierarchy and ask questions about what they are up to, who comes, what kind of events do they have or sponsor, and the levels of attendance by members and non-members. It is also very important to ask about sponsorship opportunities, which is music to their ears if you mention it first.

After the phone conversation, I generally set up a meeting with the executive director, if possible, and have a face-to-face meeting to learn even more about them and how they operate, how the board operates, how members are involved, etc. Next, I will attend a meeting or two, see who's there, ask more questions, check out what the prospects are up to and, very important, the ratio of prospects to consultants. If it's too low and the teaming opportunities aren't enough to make it worthwhile, I look for another place to spend my time. If I determine that the organization is a "keeper," I will show up diligently at every meeting, volunteer, help locate speakers for events (hopefully from my own company), and actively seek to be involved – including becoming a major sponsor of the organization and events.

No one will ever tell you it's "pay to play," but it is, so just bite the bullet and write the check and get value for your money. If you have multiple organizations to cover, every one of them should have a consistent face from your firm, one person who is known, who is always there, and with whom everyone associates instantly with your firm whenever they see them. With these criteria in mind, you will need to make sure that whoever is focused on this activity understands the real importance, because however they act will reflect directly on how your firm is perceived. Invading isn't for the floater. It is for the competitive swimmer who will dive in and swim to win. Hanging on to the side of the boat won't get it done.

Story Time:

We decided that New York City would be a great place to do business. Lots of very large projects with incredibly complicated underground conditions and huge engineering hurdles. So off to New York I went to see what's up and who's doing what with whom. Prior to going, I called the area executive director of a national urban planning organization in Philadelphia with whom I had a very nice relationship and where we had been involved and asked if she could do an introduction of me to her counterpart, a gentleman in New York, which she gladly did. I called, got an appointment, and had a very nice chat with him and discussed a number of things, including sponsorships. We went over to meet the executive director with an engineer from our fledgling New York office. It was a very interesting meeting.

The sponsorship chair for the organization was there and just happened to work for one of the largest developers in the city as a senior project manager. We had a great time and agreed to become a sponsor at whatever level I could get approved and said our goodbyes. Subsequently, we became a gold level sponsor, secured a number of meetings with the developer, and eventually started to develop business with them and had the opportunity to sponsor and participate in some educational events in the New York City area that had a real impact on our visibility. We are now working for this developer who does literally billions of dollars of business. It all started by having a plan and working it. Remember a lot of companies won't pay for memberships dues or event fees unless you serve on a committee and get involved.

The lesson: Show up. Offer to help. Get involved. Reap the benefits.

Application:

1) Make a list of every single organization that you and others in your firm are members of.
2) Take this list and see if you can find the person who is connected to that particular organization.
3) See where the gaps are.
4) Identify the organizations that have the highest percentage of prospects/clients as members.
5) Have a conversation about targeting just those organizations.

Business Development for Professionals

Bite #8
Networking-Schmoozing

Ninety percent of success in life is just showing up. This truism is at the heart of all networking. There have been scores of books written about how to, when to, where to, to whom to, but little has been written about why to, and that's what I would like to address. Why? As with all business development activities, the right attitude is fundamentally important to being successful and the right attitude begins with the right beliefs and values.

I will start with a couple of statements: (1) networking for networking's sake is a colossal waste of time; and (2) being seen to be seen is vanity at best and stupidity at worst. The heart of effective networking that is both enjoyable and productive rests in the desire to be of service to others.

This motivation is the same fundamental philosophy that underpins all truly effective business development activities, and it's just as important here.

Previously, we discussed invading an organization. I'd like to broaden this a bit and discuss effective networking on a very practical level by asking you to answer some very basic questions:
- What markets are you currently in or where do you want to be?
- Where do your existing clients from these markets congregate?
- What organizations are they members of?
- Where are your strategic team members and what organizations do they belong to?

In other words, in the markets within which you currently operate and the ones into which you want to expand, where are the clients and team members who could potentially invite you into the orbit of their clients or prospects and help you get involved with their major organizations? So much time can be wasted in rooms full of very interesting people with whom you will never do any business or from whom you will never get a lead.

I've been to major marketing organization meetings that are full of business development and marketing professionals and no clients. Don't get me wrong, some really strong relationships can be formed and potential team members identified, but these meetings are marginally influential on your success in business development. Go where the clients **and** team members are and make it your focus to help your friends, asking questions, sharing leads and developing relationships. Remember that people do business with people they like, so be likable.

If you're a professional who does not either want to do this or one that doesn't have the time, hire someone who does and really likes to do it. Don't feel badly if you don't like to network and be out and about. It may not be you and that's equally important to recognize. Just realize that for your firm to be successful someone needs to keep their eye on this ball, be out there in the marketplace, be visible and exposed to all the potential opportunities, and be consistent at it.

William C. Johnson

Just remember this truism: *sporadic business development isn't*. True business development is a long-term commitment to grow and maintain relationships and visibility. Make a measureable commitment. X breakfasts, Y dinners, Z lunches and mix it up between evening and morning events.

Story time:

I attended a major college and university planners' conference in Pittsburgh with a strategic business partner, and while we were there, we invited a couple of our existing clients to dinner. My architect friend invited a couple of his clients too. The dinner was planned a month in advance and coordinated with all the guests. The thought was to get our clients together to meet with each other, form some relationships and give us a chance to interact with them also. The evening was a great success. Not only did we get to meet some new clients, as did our architect friend, we were also able to offer our assistance to put together (and present at) a one-day, subject-focused event later that year on one of the campuses that was represented that night.

We have subsequently developed a great relationship with both of the schools to which we were introduced and have begun work on both of the campuses. Our architect friend has subsequently been invited to present on the two campuses and has continued discussions with the two clients we brought along. Everyone in the room was helped in one way or another. This effort was associated with a targeted conference, lots of clients and prospects and high quality team members. Our networking was focused and revolved around cementing personal relationships and helping people with issues that they were facing. Success and happiness ensued.

William C. Johnson

Bite #9
Conferences

You've found an organization or a couple of them that are packed with potential clients and team members, you've gone to some meetings, chatted with the executive director, learned about what they are all about, and you've determined that it's worth spending some more time and testing the waters.

With any new organization, I like to go to an event as just a participant if possible: no exhibit or display or sponsorship. My plan is fairly simple. I research the previous year's attendees', if available, to determine who's been attending and check to see if there are any current clients whom I could call and ask about their thoughts and reactions to the conference. If I can't get an attendees list from the organization, I'll find one of my friends who was there as a sponsor or attendee and I'll ask them for the list. With a little persistence you can find almost anything out!

I also look at the vendor/partners list to see who might be displaying, call a few of them if I know them well enough, and ask how they liked the previous conferences. With the attendee list in hand for the conference, I research them and come up with a list of potential people that I want to meet and keep those names handy. Prior to the conference, I take the schedule and see what tracks or series of presentations they are offering and try to attend a series of sessions across the tracks in hopes of meeting as many different people as I can.

You should also see who's presenting to see if there are either specific clients or strategic partners who might be worth a visit. If you stick with one track, you'll see most of the same faces, so spread yourself around.

Now you're at the conference. Rule #1 is to go to every event from beginning to end and circulate. Sit at different tables in the morning for coffee, lunch, dinner. As with any event, sit down at tables that have people there already and be ready to engage. Show up early if nametags are being given out to check to see who's there but don't sit down first. Let the room partially fill up to see if you can strategically find people you wanted to sit with once they are in place.

Here's a tip on name tags. Clip it on your right lapel or on the right side of your shirt so it is easier to read while you're shaking hands. Have it in a conspicuous place so that someone doesn't have to search your upper body looking for it. Also, don't sit with your friends or people from your firm. Split up and cover the room.

If there is an exhibit hall, work it completely during the times that it's open. Most exhibitors will be glad to chat. That is why they are there, so make the most of it. Learn about the quality of the convening organization from their perspective. Ask about previous conferences and how well they were attended. Inquire about the requirements for submitting winning presentations at them, and see who might be a strategic team member based on what you are learning. While you're there, you will get a chance to listen to a variety of these professionals discussing what they do, how they do it and the associated benefits to potential clients (if they're doing it right!). Listen in. It is a great way to learn.

When you attend the presentations, take a moment to speak with the presenters and just ask them how they were able to secure a spot. Have they spoken at this conference in the past? How did they structure their abstracts to get noticed? Are there any particular formats that are preferred?

Another thought on presentations. Check to see if any of the presenters are potential clients and are on your "hit" list. If they are place yourself near the front of the room and pay attention. After the presentation go up immediately prior to the crush and introduce yourself, give them your constructive feedback and get a card and ask if you could follow up with them. This is a great way to get through to hard to contact people who are almost unreachable behind multiple gatekeepers, voicemail and spam guard!

Conferences are expensive and to make the most out of them, I always try to secure a spot to speak for our teams. Having a speaking slot is one of the most advantageous places to be. It is rare that you won't get business from presenting.

I have found that you won't get selected unless you have a satisfied client on the presentation team and, if they are capable of being the lead presenter, have them do the lion's share of the presentation. The less the audience sees of you, the higher likelihood that you'll get good leads from this effort. Let your client sell you. Remember less is always more.

Presentations usually come with an unspoken price tag of sponsorship. No one would ever admit this, but it's the way it is, and it's worth it if you are at the right conference with the right people.

So now you have done the conference, returned to the office, figured out your expense report, and answered 4,000 emails. What's next?

I like to sit down right away, grab my notes and the conference brochure, and do a report for people at the firm to let them know what I learned, what's new, who I met (both potential clients and team members), and who I will be following up with and how. This is a good time to check and see if anyone else in the firm has had contact with your new list for any history that might be important. I also take a moment to reflect on the value of the event in relation to visibility with our client groups. Then the follow-up work begins with emails, telephone calls and, hopefully, a list of excellent appointments and the possibility of working with great new clients.

Story Time:

If you lose your sense of humor, you are done. Go home, go play golf, take the day off.

I was attending a large regional conference that I had been working for years – a premier organization full of clients and great strategic partners. We had presented at this conference multiple times on a variety of projects and subjects with our clients, and we were a completely entrenched and known quantity.

The opening night of the exhibit hall is one of the main events. Everyone is happy, having cocktails, munching on great finger food, and touring the hall looking at all the great displays. Mine was the only booth without one because the conference company misplaced all my supplies, literature and my 8 by 10 booth with all the really cool graphics. All I had were my business cards and a fish bowl to collect cards for a giveaway, which was also missing, go figure.

Well, when life hands you lemons you make lemonade. I stood there and told everyone that I was being sustainable and that I was the only one in attendance with a completely carbon-neutral booth. All my friends came by to laugh at me and brought more people with them. Well, as it worked out, everyone was so amused with the situation, they all came by to commiserate, and I wound up speaking with more people than ever.

My booth did show up the next morning at 6 AM. I got it set up and operational for the next day, and then people all came back to see how I'd made out. It turned out to be a really good show. I kept my cool and got to know all the people from the local organization who were hosting the event. They felt terrible and all the conference set-up people were mortified that they had lost my stuff. Everything happens for a reason. You just have to figure out how to adapt!

Application:

Do some internal interviews about the conferences your firm has attended in the past and, if possible, speak with a group of trusted clients and partners for their impressions of really effective conferences. See if you can find any reports or attendance lists. Do your homework on the conferences you've attended and develop a "perfect conference" template to give yourself an idea of what it would look like, Then compare it to what you've been doing. Does it match?

Business Development for Professionals

Bite #10
Reporting from the Front

William C. Johnson

I just want to take another moment on reporting in general. In the last "bite" I discussed reporting on your conference activities and the things you learned right after you get back. Reporting on business development activities is important for a couple of reasons. The most important one is that it makes sure that your co-workers and management know what you are doing and how you are spending the precious business development dollars being allocated to your efforts. These reports don't have to be tomes. Keep them brief so that people will actually read them, which is the point.

A very simple business development format that I've used for years is a look back/forward-one month report. I simply go to my favorite client-relationship-management system and look back one month and track down all the major events and appointments that I had, and then I look forward a month and do the same thing.

If you prefer, you can also use this report as a way to invite others in your company to go along with you. If they see something in the schedule that they might like to assist with, they can get back to you about attending; it's just a way of engaging on the inside.

I will warn you that there are those who will look at this activity as self-promotion. My answer to that is "so what?" Business development can be fairly invisible on the inside and that can be career-limiting, so take some time and make sure that people know what you're doing!

Just one more point. Really make an effort to get other people in your firm engaged with these reports. Post them on your intranet page, send them to strategic people in the firm who are the thought leaders. Make them and yourself visible.

William C. Johnson

Bite #11
Stories

I don't know about the rest of you, but I really learn and relate when people explain things to me using an example of where it's worked before for someone in a similar situation. Think about the people around you, and see if you can target the ones who like to tell stories about what they did last weekend, what their kids are doing, where they're going on vacation – you know, stories! Well, stories are an extremely powerful and under-used weapon in the arsenal of business development, and if you really want to get better at it, you must collect them and use them effectively.

Collecting stories is fun. Here's how you go about it. Get up from your desk and ask your co-workers what they've done recently to meet or exceed client/customer expectations. Ask them to explain in some detail exactly what they did, how they did it and what the results were.

My guess is that if you ask about five senior/mid-level people in your office this question, you will have plenty of ammunition to use in conversations out in "client land" when someone asks you the question "Gee, what do you guys do anyway?" You come back with a story about how your firm helped someone just like them with a particular problem and what the resolution was, which will point out the benefit to them.

There is another way to collect stories, which is a group activity, and whenever I do it, people show up. It's fun. (Business development is supposed to be fun. That is why I enjoy it.) You invite everyone to go to the conference room for a lunch time "story time" session. Sit, eat together and go around the table and have each person tell a story about what they're working on, what's unique about it, what problems they have solved, what issues came up during the process that caused hair loss and lack of sleep, and how they got over the hump.

One day, we learned that we, as a firm, were expert at counting fish as part of an environmental study. WHO KNEW! We didn't, but it was an awful lot of fun; we learned what we each were doing, and it gave all of us great illustrations to use when explaining the breadth of what we do.

During an interview with a client or a prospect, as you're listening to the answers to your questions and getting a real feel for where the client is experiencing difficulty or challenges, use the other side of your brain to go through your filing cabinet of stories and pull a couple out for illustrative purposes. Use them in the conversation, then continue with your questions.

It is extremely effective, proves you're listening and, not only that, it shows that you're processing on your feet and using real life examples of where you've helped others in similar situations. I can't stress how effective this method will be. It can be a real differentiator and an excellent way to grow a relationship.

Story Time about Story Time:

I set up a meeting between one of my co-workers and a recently acquired client. This particular client was, and is still I'm certain, extremely bright, quick-witted and intelligent, my favorite kind. We were going to this lunch date to discuss some pretty "out there" concepts in planning and the whole rationale behind doing planning in a different way than normal.

Prior to the lunch, my co-conspirator and I discussed which stories we would use. We didn't have any idea of where exactly we would use them in the conversation because we really didn't have any idea where the conversation was going to go. With this person it could go anywhere, which is in my mind always a thrill, but conversations like this can be a little unnerving for people not used to doing things "on the fly", especially if you aren't prepared.

We started with our obligatory 10 questions to get things started and used those questions to steer the conversation toward the story and we finally got there. We told the story, and the response was as we would have hoped an instant recognition of the issue and the potential for this new process to help him directly. He literally sold himself on what we were presenting to him. We really didn't do anything other than present an application of the concepts we were discussing in a real life story for him to see. He expressed an immediate desire to move forward with a proposal and designated himself as our internal champion for the process.

William C. Johnson

<u>Application</u>

1) Collect ten stories
2) Set up a story time session at lunch once a month for three months. Don't ask for permission – just do it!
3) Post the stories in note form on the company intranet or on the wall by the coffee machine.
4) Start to tell these stories to your co-workers, to get used to using them in conversation; then encourage them to do the same thing with their stories.
5) When you develop your pre-meeting planner, identify the particular stories you want to use.

Business Development for Professionals

Bite #12
Elevator Speeches

William C. Johnson

You've heard the phrase "elevator speech" but have you ever actually tried to get someone's attention, hold it and engage them in a serious conversation when you only have 15 seconds to bait the hook?

Peoples' attention spans are so short – according to various sources as short as seven seconds before they "go away" for a bit that you really need to be creative with this. In the book "The Complete Guide to Public Speaking" by Jeff Davidson it says that attention spans are at seven minutes, better than seven seconds, but still very short. You can't begin to help people if you don't get their attention, so you need to develop an expertise at becoming interested quickly.

I've heard some good ones in the past. From an environmental engineer, I heard that she "plays with hazardous waste." Or from a geotechnical engineer, "we manage risk for all the scary things going on underground."

Think about what you do – maybe as a group activity in your office – and come up with creative ideas about what you could say about it that would grab someone's attention long enough for them to think about asking a clarifying question. Then you have them at least for a couple of minutes.

Elevator speeches are very important to practice, and I encourage you to do so within the confines of your own office with each other. Try to explain what your firm does, lace it with client benefits, and do it in under a minute. As uncomfortable as it might be for some people, role playing is a very productive and useful tool for learning new interpersonal skills. These role plays might be between two individuals while others watch, or you actually might split into teams and run the scenarios. However you decide to rehearse, remember that practice in a safe environment makes perfect and that perfecting your first contact with others is worth its weight in gold. Remember, you never have a second chance to make a first impression.

Story Time:

I'm in an elevator going to the top floor at a function for a very nice organization in Rhode Island. Riding with me is a gentleman who recognizes my company name on my tag, and he asks me what we do. I have exactly five floors to get this done. I say, "We do scary underground engineering projects." He smiles and asks me as we leave the elevator what I mean by that, and he lists off about six different kinds of projects that he would consider difficult underground engineering situations. I agree that that's what we do.

Now that I have him, I use a couple of stories where we've done very unique work and saved our clients time, material and money.

After a series of meetings, we started to work for this client, and since then we've done a number of projects for them.

William C. Johnson

Application:

1) Develop your speech.
2) Practice with others in your office.
3) Make a pact that you will tell someone your speech at least once a day.
4) Develop multiple pitches for multiple purposes.
5) Start to attach stories to your elevator speeches that are relevant to illustrate your points and have them ready!

Business Development for Professionals

Bite #13
Qualification Process

Qualification is the vetting process that you will start at the very beginning of the whole business development/sales process to determine if the company you've identified as a potential client meets your criteria for the long-term, and it always involves lots of questions.

All of us have a variety of internal systems for tracking "leads" and, in some cases, proposal numbers or prospect numbers are assigned very early in the process. I would offer that prospective clients shouldn't be entered into any systems until they are at least initially qualified as a suitable fit. What do I mean by qualified?

This process begins with the first contact you have with the prospect –whether in person, on the phone, by email, when you're doing your initial research on the web, or checking with your network to see who knows anything about the individual or company. The qualification process is very hard to codify because, at this stage in the whole business development process, very little is really known about the prospect – and the likelihood or the desire to have them as a client.

You are really trying to find out what their perceived and real needs are, how they match up with what you have to offer, and generally what is the possibility for having a long-lasting, cooperative and fruitful relationship with this client. Researching the kinds of projects that they do or are involved with can be a valuable tool for qualifying a prospect, as can identifying the businesses that they normally team up with. If by chance they have mutual contacts with someone you know, a well-placed call can be invaluable. If it's a prospect who has done business with one of your team members, that call can be very fruitful and might even result in an introduction in person, on the phone, or maybe on the golf course!

By spending quality time researching your own business and evaluating the most successful client relationships in your book of business, you will begin to develop a profile of the clients you should be seeking out and the questions you may want to ask to determine if they are a "fit." The goal here is to have a process that's not rigid, but very fluid and one that quickly separates the sheep from the goats so that you're not wasting valuable time and resources.

The same holds true for team members that have the potential of being leverage points for greater opportunity. What sort of team members/strategic partners have worked well with your organization in the past? What is their profile, if you can determine that? If you can, you have a valuable tool with which to separate the people you should be cultivating and those with whom you shouldn't spend too much time.

By applying a qualification process at the earliest stages of the business development cycle you can save valuable time, and the information gained can bring clarity and certainty to your go/no-go decision making process.

William C. Johnson

<u>Story Time:</u>

I attended a conference for college and university business officers and had the opportunity to meet a number of potential clients. One person that I met initially introduced himself to me as coming from a very small community college system in Pennsylvania. I thought to myself, "How long will I let this conversation go on before I politely excuse myself?" But I hung in there and decided to qualify this person and make sure that there wasn't something that we had to offer him. I asked him what energy and sustainability planning looked like at his campus, and he went on for a while. I asked him what kind of master planning activities he was involved with and he went on again. And then I asked him what his responsibilities included in his department, and he told me that he was responsible for the design and construction activities for forty-two community college campuses.

Maybe he wanted to see if I'd just stick with him, but by doing so I learned this important information, and I was glad that I'd stayed engaged. You never know until you've fully engaged, gone through as many questions as you need to, and satisfied yourself definitively whether it's real or not.

Application

1) Develop five relevant questions that you would ask during a qualification interview and the answers that would be expected from a perfect client.
2) If you don't know these five questions, go ask a principal at the firm what they would be.
3) Use them at your next meeting and test them out.

William C. Johnson

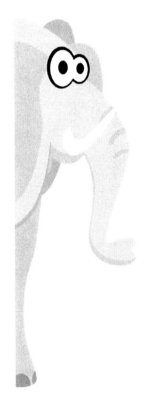

Bite #14
Setting up Meetings

Setting up meetings is part of the business development process and also part of the actual sales process, which can be separate and distinct phase. In sales, you are trying to get to "yes." You are trying to get to "yes" on multiple occasions on multiple subjects, but you are trying to add up all the "yeses" to one big one.

One of the first "yeses" happens when the prospect agrees to have a meeting with you to sit and discuss their needs, wants, and requirements, a meeting at which you are going to ask questions, listen and speak as little as possible – remember two ears and one mouth – and listen twice as much. So, how do we go about getting that fateful first meeting and make sure that it's not "fatal?"

Here's a process that works for me. Feel free to modify it any way that feels comfortable. Do your research and collect all your notes from previous contacts with the prospect, maybe from that conference or trade show. If you have had at least some initial contact, this step is easier because, hopefully, you planted some seeds that you can now water. Was there a subject that he really wanted to hear about? Was there mention of an issue or problem that he was dealing with during a project that you heard during your conversation? You are looking for something to put on the hook to get this first meeting. If there is a particularly unique service offering that you couldn't cover during your first informal meeting, it might be a place from which to start.

I usually start with a simple, short email where I state the fact, conversationally, that it was nice to have met them and that I wanted to follow up with targeted additional information, and that I had specific questions for them about a particular item we discussed. I tell them that I will be in touch with them in the next two weeks by phone and then that's what I do. I call, it's semi-warm at this point, and give them two dates that I can make it to a meeting. Giving them two dates puts them in charge and works quite well at transferring apparent control to them.

This approach is for someone that you've met, and sometimes it can take awhile with how busy people are, but if you are pleasantly persistent you will get in to see them. We will discuss shortly what you're going to do then.

For dead cold calls, it's a little more complicated. You need to do considerably more research on your offerings and try to determine where on their radar screen you may fall. Do they have other suppliers who are your competitors? Are they in the middle of (or, better still, planning) a major project where your services may be valuable? Are there particular regulatory or legal hurdles that are confronting their industry where you could help? Do your research prior to calling because you've got about 20 seconds to tell them why it's important for them to listen even if you send an introductory email, which I always do.

Same procedure, send the email and follow up. If they happened to open up the conversation with the email, that's great because you can follow this along, collect more information and possibly get passed to the right person. Keep everything you say or do short and to the point. Watch your grammar and spelling and keep it professional.

If you're not successful at getting emails or voicemails returned, here are a couple of other ideas. Ask the personal assistant some questions about the department, just informational kind of things, and build some rapport with them – you know how to do this. Ask them if they keep their boss's calendar – if yes, ask them if they could schedule you in if no, ask them when is a good time to call to catch her in – early, late, lunch?

I will try people right after 7 a.m., right before lunch, literally 11:55 a.m., and at around 4:45 p.m. If I know they are early birds from my conversation with the administrative assistant, I will call them even earlier, at their desks, not on their cell phone. The reason I don't call them on their cell phones is that I don't know them yet and sometimes even if you have their cell phone number it's not always wise to use it. If they've forwarded their office phones to their cell that's great, but you never know.

Once you get the meeting scheduled always, always confirm it the day before. It's polite and can save you valuable time and effort showing up and being forgotten or bumped. It also gives you another excuse to speak with them, even if it's only for a couple of minutes.

William C. Johnson

Story Time

This story is going to be a little different. Making cold calls can be extremely intimidating for all of us. But there are mitigation techniques if you want to get better, and it starts and ends with practice.

If there is a person in your office who makes a lot of calls – cold, warm or dead – ask them if you could just listen in while they are making them. I've done it and found it be very useful. You can sit someone in a conference room and tell them to make cold calls and give them all the techniques and the questions, but they still are locked up when it comes to doing them. You wouldn't teach your kid to ride a bike this way, would you? Well, you can't expect someone to learn how to do this without showing them.

I had the opportunity to work with a couple of very bright and engaging young engineers who really wanted to learn how to do this, so I said "OK, team, here's what we're going to do. You're going to get on a conference call with me and mute your phones and listen in while I make some cold calls, how's that?" Well, that was fine with them.

This process is like reality TV – "BD Survivor" – and you have absolutely no idea what's going to happen. It could be really good or really bad, or really, really bad. As it turned out, it went well, and, by showing them that it wasn't the end of the world if you didn't get it all absolutely correct, it enabled them to pick up the phone themselves. I would encourage you to either show someone how to do it, if you know how, or find someone who knows how and ask them to give you some live mentoring. It worked quite well and was actually kind of amusing getting critiqued by some junior staff. "Why did you say that?" "So that's how you get through the gate keeper, who knew?" It wasn't dull!

Application:

1) Find someone, if you aren't the one, who can actually show you how it's done – how to make these cold calls – so that you can listen in and get a feel for it.
2) If you are the business development professional in your office and you have some disciples, try this exercise with them and see if it doesn't enable them to pick the phone up.

William C. Johnson

Bite #15
Preparing for Meetings

Previously, we discussed in the discovery "bite" how we are essentially on a fact-finding mission early in the BD process. We need to categorically deny knowing anything about the prospect, so that we don't assume we know about their particular situation. There is nothing worse than making a statement that you assume is correct and having to backtrack in the first meeting.

So, you have the first meeting set up. Now you need to prepare. I use a pre-meeting planner that I put together. It's a very simple, one-page outline of who's coming, where are they on the corporate organization chart, what major issues we should be discussing with them, and the ten questions I am going to start with. If it's an unfamiliar industry or client type, I try to find someone internally who has had some experience with the type of company, and run my questions past them to make sure that I'm on the right track.

Once I have finalized the questions, I will just take a couple of minutes to actually practice saying them out loud to see how they sound. You'd be amazed how smoothly you will be able to deliver them if you just take that couple of minutes and repeat them to make sure that they are conversational and sound that way. Remember, you don't have to sound brilliant, but you do need to sound interested and informed. The questions should all be open-ended starting with who, why, what, how or when. You don't want them to be able to respond with one word answers, but in a manner that gives you a thorough explanation. If you are able to get into this sort of rhythm and maintain it for ten to 15 minutes, you'll be amazed at the information you will be able to collect.

Eventually they will want to know more about what you do, the services you offer and whom you've worked with, and you will be armed with specific information from this process to tailor your responses.

The pre-meeting planner is also a great tool if more than one person from your firm is going to accompany you at the meeting. It will give you the opportunity to share the questions between the two of you and figure out who's going to ask what. This approach will tell the prospect that you're working as a team, which is always a good thing, and it also will give you a chance to ask questions that you can comment on from your particular area of expertise.

I take the pre-meeting planner with me to the meeting and make notes on it, and later I add this information to the client relationship management database or to my notes. Faithful use of a pre-meeting planner will also lower your anxiety about doing these meetings in the first place. You have a specific plan going into the meeting. What can go wrong? It's been thought out and practiced. You have a goal in mind and a path to get there. You have enough questions to ask for a 30 to 45 minute interview, and you don't have to worry about dead air or having to talk too much.

If you need to actually practice this active interview technique, try doing so with a fellow team member until you are comfortable. If you really want to hone this talent, set up a video camera and take turns and actually critique each other and practice being different types of prospects. I know that this process doesn't sound like much fun, but it can be highly effective. Remember that the reason we're using this kind of a tool is to make the process as predictable and productive as possible, which hopefully will reduce your stress and make the process just that much more enjoyable.

Story Time:

Going out on joint interviews with people in your office can sometimes feel a little out of control if the other people are not accomplished listeners. I've had success with using the pre-meeting planner as a tool to control my own team. We have gone out, and everyone had specific instructions to ask their questions and record the answers. I ran a series of internal business development training sessions at our firm, and for months after my graduates would call me to review their pre-meeting planners just to go over the questions and try them out. I would encourage you to do the same with your team. Share your questions and the process, and use it as a way to bring more people up to speed on how this valuable tool can be used to positively influence you as you discover your clients' and prospects' needs, wants and desires.

William C. Johnson

Application:

1) Develop a pre-meeting template for your team to use on every preliminary meeting.
2) Develop a list of pre-meeting questions, specific to the client type, and write them down.
3) Try this template out on an existing client just for practice.
4) Practice makes perfect: as you start to use this form it will quickly become second nature.

Business Development for Professionals

Bite #16
Meeting Goals

William C. Johnson

As part of your pre-meeting planner, you should spend time thinking about potential outcomes and possible directions the meeting could take, so that you can prepare as thoroughly as possible. As you move through the meeting, it may become apparent that you need to spend more time on a particular subject that comes up – and that you and your fellow team member aren't the best resource to explain it as thoroughly as possible.

This is not a negative, but actually a very positive situation. It immediately opens up the opportunity for another meeting where the subject can be handled in greater detail by the right person, whom you will bring along to that session, and you can ask for and set the next meeting up right then.

Another outcome might be your offer to send along more descriptive literature regarding the topics and issues discussed, preferably project case studies illustrating valuable solutions for clients! These days, I try to do this with electronic files to save paper, carbon emissions, and money –and people seem to appreciate it. When I do send information, I will also offer to call and review it with the prospect.

Working lunch or brown-bag sessions-during which you can provide in-depth information to them and their staff about a particular subject – can be very useful. If they express interest in having such a session, discuss it, come up with specific ideas, give them a brief overview/agenda of what you are planning, and then get back to them with some potential dates. We will discuss this more in the webinar bite.

Of course, the very best result of this meeting would be a request to put your services into a proposal aimed at addressing a need or needs that you've uncovered with the prospective client. If that's the case, you may want to spend time reviewing a proposed scope of work with them in some detail to make certain that you walk away with a thorough understanding of what they want. If there's a white board, step up and start the outlining process right then and there.

Doing this "live" is a great way to show your competence and grasp of the situation. If I sense that the prospect has a real interest regarding what we've been discussing, I will offer a proposal to them as a way to move the conversation forward. Don't mail proposals unless absolutely necessary; instead, take them to the prospect and review them in person. This approach gives you another reason to get in front of them, establish a connection, and further build the relationship. It also shows responsiveness and empathy, both of which are at the top of any list in attributes prized by clients.

William C. Johnson

Bite #17
The Meeting

Be conversational, smile, don't rush, pay attention, and start with something light. Being the active listener is an extremely powerful position to lead a meeting from, moving the agenda and remaining in control.

Try starting with; "What did you do last weekend?" "Have you been to any conferences lately for XYZ organization?" "How's your golf game?" Use whatever you want just to get things going. Have a leading question to get the conversation going, and let the person complete their thoughts. Have your questions laid out in your mind and on your planner so that they will direct the conversation in a logical sequence to where you'd like it to go.

Bring some humor into the conversation if you can and it's appropriate. It can really help with creating a pleasant mood. Remember, if you really want to know what's motivating, driving or really concerning people, ask "why" questions consecutively (consider the industry adage that it takes five responses to "why" to get to the core of an issue). The prospect says, "we're really struggling with our internal strategic planning." You say, "Why is it such a struggle for your firm?" They answer, and you ask why again. If it's comfortable and you aren't making them crazy with this technique you will have probably arrive at the heart of the issue. This is just a technique to blend in, if appropriate. You can actually try this on co-workers if you'd like to see how it works. It's very effective at defusing potentially adversarial situations, if used discreetly.

I've also found that lunches or coffee can be a great way to meet with people where it can be more casual. Taking notes is fine. Just be aware of how it affects your attention to the client or prospect. If you are prone to taking verbatim notes, leave your pen at home.

The key to a good meeting is to do your pre-meeting planner, understand your prospect by doing your homework, have your questions ready, and have two or three stories related to what you're going to be talking about that you can share at appropriate times to illustrate your value. These types of interrogatory interviews are the heart of business development, whether they happen with a client, prospect, or a business partner.

Becoming an expert interviewer is the quickest way to be seen as professional and empathetic. You will be viewed as someone who really cares and wants to get all the information and then develop appropriate actions based on what you've learned.

Business Development for Professionals

Bite #18
Follow Up

William C. Johnson

Persisting without crossing the line to becoming a distraction to be avoided can be a hard line to toe, and occasionally you will cross over it, but there are some things you can do to protect yourself from doing it very often. Once you have done the meeting and followed up with literature or a telephone call or even a proposal, you have to wait – and sometimes you have to wait a long time. Steady and professional persistence can pay off in the long run, but you must be as patient as a saint sometimes.

Adjust your tactics to every situation based upon your intuitive feel for the prospect and how hard you think they may perceive you are pushing. Remember, it is their perception with which you are concerned, not yours. After the initial meeting and follow-up, I will wait at least two weeks and follow up with a phone call, and if I get their voicemail leave them a very brief message stating that I was just following up to answer any questions they may have had. I will have the same brief conversation, if perchance I actually get them on the phone. After this I will give them a month, then three, then six.

If it was a particularly good prospect where I think we could really help them, I will go out of my way to find interesting, timely articles in trade journals, magazines or on organizational websites and send them along, with just a brief note, and keep touching base with them periodically. Quality business development cycles can be years in the making. Persistence and patience are key components. I have been impatient, and it <u>never</u> works; ouch! If you remember that you are focusing on helping them identify and solve their problem(s) – not on selling for selling's sake – you can be better able to strike the right tone as your proposal is evaluated and escalated through the prospect's company.

<u>Story Time:</u>

A particular university had been on my list of potential clients for at least five years. At conferences and symposiums for all of those years I had met with various members of the facilities design, construction, and planning management and staff. We had multiple meetings regarding our services and what we could do to assist them with their campus planning activities. Yet we couldn't seem to gain traction.

We'd developed what we thought were unique and compelling service offerings with superior benefits, but still made no forward progress. We had invited them to our seminars, webinars and conference presentations, and they came. There were still no signs of progress, but I persisted.

One of my favorite sayings – and I think I coined this one myself - is: "If you're everywhere all the time you're bound to be at the right place some of the time." Well, I needed to meet the senior campus planner (whom I'd never met previously) and knew he would be at a particular conference, so I went with the primary goal of meeting him. And I did: in the food line for dinner.

William C. Johnson

He proved to be a great guy who was very bright and really liked to talk, so I let him talk, and after about an hour of listening to him and asking him questions, he finally turned the tables and asked me about myself and my company. Well, we spent that dinner together and then he spent the next day with me, and I introduced him around. He had the opportunity to listen to me as I explained what we did as a firm to others that I met wandering around this conference. He was very complimentary of the way that I approached others through using questions and basically interviewing them on the fly.

At the end of that conference and after a couple of drinks and dinners, we had the beginnings of a good relationship; we knew about each other's families and where we liked to vacation and what we were both trying to accomplish in our positions. He had an honesty that was very easy to deal with. At this point, I thought, "Gee, this looks pretty good; we'll probably be on campus by like next week!" Not so fast.. It was another year, more calls and meetings, but in the end we were on campus as a real member of the team and uniquely helping them solve their problems.

It took about five years to turn them into a client, but it was absolutely worth it. And we should have them as a client for a long time based on the time and trust that was developed during all those years.

Business Development for Professionals

Bite #19
Constant Contact

It is a real challenge to stay in contact with all the high-value people on your list without being viewed as being over-zealous. You want to stay in touch with people and stay on their radar screen, keeping your business card on the top of their pile, so that when needs arise you're one of the first people they think to call. Here are a couple of suggestions based upon my experience and that of others I know.

The first one is the easiest, and it's for all your strategic team members, the people you team with most frequently on projects. Sharing leads on new work that you've developed or new technology or techniques are great ways to stay in touch and be viewed as a real, true partner. If you share leads with your team members and they secure work from taking advantage of this market intelligence, you will be on the top of their lists of firms that they will turn to. Also, keep in mind that you can take market information that you've personally developed and share it with people from non-competitive industries. This technique has never failed to generate tangible good will and bring more information back to me.

Other methods you can use: just call and check in, go to lunch, play a round of golf with someone whom you know, and invite someone that they'd like to meet. This approach works even better if the person you invite is a potential client that your team member has been trying to get in front of, and through your relationship you can be the one to connect them.

This sharing of information and contacts is an excellent relationship-building tool if you can make it happen. Everyone is happy in this situation by your helping two people who need to know each other have a chance to meet in an informal, non-threatening atmosphere.

I use another method to stay in touch: once a quarter (or so) I'll put together a newsy email and send it to a segment of my address book of team members to just let them know what I'm doing, where we've been, what's new that we're learning. This email is to just check in and that's actually the title of my email…"Checking In." I have never had a bad response, and, more often than not, people will respond and fill me in on their latest news. It's kind of your own social network (without all the e-hype).

With prospective clients, it can be a little more difficult to not be seen as a pest, which is always a risk. If I see news stories relating to their industry in a magazine or on the internet, I'll send them a copy or a link. If I learn specific high quality market intelligence or have a question for them, I'll drop them a note or an email just to keep in contact. I've found the sharing of relevant information with them the best way of doing this, so I stay up-to-date on trade journals, web pages on their industry, and other relevant publications. Reading what they read is a good way to keep your finger on the pulse of potential issues that they face – and to be more responsive.

William C. Johnson

Story Time

We had a major institutional client that was very influential and on everyone's "hit list." They happened to be our client and one of my golfing partners. During a conversation one day, it became apparent to me that this particular client needed some engineering and planning assistance that was not part of our normal service offerings. It also became apparent to me through a series of questions that there had been a string of people in the recent past that hadn't "made the grade."

I offered to have one of our strategic partners contact this client to discuss the specific situation with which they were dealing and see if there might be a potential for the two of them to work together. The client agreed, so I made the call, and the contact was made. Well, the strategic partner was all that the client hoped they would be; they were retained and did a fine job on the project which made both of us look good. They are still engaged with this client and going strong.

Now, how pleased do you think this strategic partner was? He was *ecstatic*, and it has deepened his firm's trust in ours and has resulted in multiple projects being directed to us. Was this hard to do? No, it wasn't because, at its core, I was serving my client's best interests. Sometimes the best thing you can do is to recognize that you can't do something and turn it around in a creative fashion. You have the opportunity with your relationships to leverage your own business success, and you must always be thinking about and making connections.

William C. Johnson

Bite #20
Presentations

Many excellent books and articles have been written about how to prevent "death by powerpoint". YouTube videos have been shot about the tragic consequences of presentations gone bad, very bad.

I am not going to go into a long treatise on how to put together effective presentations, but I will give you a very succinct list:

- Create a visual, memorable moment right away.
- Ask polling questions of the audience to engage them after every two or three slides.
- Create anticipation by being a little controversial.
- Capture their attention.
- Try to create conflict in their minds with alternative thoughts.
- Pose questions that go against commonly held beliefs and methods.
- Use graphics frequently and appropriately.
- Try to create an entire presentation with no words (try it and see what happens).
- If you do use words six-point font and you read the slides verbatim, go to the nearest window, open it, and jump out; it will leave a far more lasting impression than what you were doing originally.
- Figure about three minutes per slide and – unless asked to go longer – keep your presentation to about 20 minutes.
- If you are making points on slides, put a maximum of three lines per slide and just enough words to drive your narrative.

William C. Johnson

- Did I already *say "don't read the slides?"*...well, don't...it's deadly...someone can die...like you!

Presentations are supposed to be engaging so engage and don't lecture. Remember to smile and try to walk around the room. Don't hide behind the podium, and don't play with your pen or jingle the change in your pocket or say "um" and "ah" every three words.

Of all the things that you absolutely need to do, it is to <u>practice</u>. I have seen hundreds of presentations, and I can tell immediately if the person has taken the time to practice. The first thing I notice is whether the presenter can introduce themselves without stumbling. If it starts with a stumble, you usually have someone who hasn't practiced and the rest of the presentation is likely to be more than a little rough.

The next presentation you hear, keep this critique in mind and see what kind of an indicator it is. Knowing this issue, critique yourself and <u>practice</u>. I know you don't enjoy standing up in front of your office mates and practicing, but it matters so much I want you to do it anyway; do the whole presentation at least <u>three</u> times. If you will follow this regimen, you will develop such confidence in yourself and your material that you will incorporate it into your normal routine, allowing a smooth flow to your presentation, more like a conversation than a lecture. And on the "um's"... When you practice, consciously catch yourself or have someone else "ding" you to break the habit. Being silent while you collect your thoughts is fine, using "um" as a silence-filler makes you look unsure of yourself so break this habit.

If you incorporate these ideas into your skill development and really practice you will be on auto pilot *Michael Jordan was so driven to be great, and worked so hard at it, that he practiced and worked on his game over and over again, and it became part of his muscle memory, so when he made one of his amazing moves, and it appeared to spontaneous, he in fact did NOT have to think about what he was doing at that moment, but had trained himself so specifically that he could do those things without thinking, without letting his head (doubt) get in the way.*

If you will commit to this same regimen when you get to the prospect's conference room and you won't even have to think. You will stand and deliver and you will sound great. I understand that this process may feel hard to do, but I encourage you to try it and see whether it makes it easier.

And with all presentations remember the age-old axiom: tell them what you are going to tell them, tell them, and then tell them what you told them. There is a great little book entitled "Presentations Plus" by an old IBM'er. He's got the skinny tie, looks like a complete dork, but he really has great insight. If you really want to excel at it, pick up a good book on the subject and practice what you learn.

William C. Johnson

Bite #21
WebEx-Webinars-E-vitations

OK – you have developed some really great presentations, you've made some wonderful connections through client organizations and associations, you've got an electronic address book that would choke a whale, and now you want to combine all of it into a very impactful business development campaign. There are a couple of options to consider, and I'll start with the simplest one.

Webinars are a great way to share information, save money on travel, and reduce your carbon footprint. We've found them to be very well received for lunch time sessions where people can just sit at their desks and participate. It's also a great way to practice presentations without having to actually stand up in front of an audience. We've used them with prospects, clients and team members, and for internal training, and I recommend becoming expert at using this medium.

Professional webinars for larger groups are a bit more difficult and need targeted and closer communication and oversight for them to go off without a hitch. If you have a particular subject that you'd like to get out to a group of your clients and prospects, it can be a very effective method if it is structured and administered properly.

One of the keys I've found is to have a client who's already been involved with the service offering being discussed play an integral part in the presentation, so that the others are hearing it from a peer. Webinars should be closely coordinated with administrative staff familiar with the technology and how to effectively interface with the participants.

You also need to design an effective follow-up campaign so that any questions or leads that are generated are not lost and people who have expressed interest are contacted promptly. These sessions need to be practiced multiple times with scripts if necessary to keep everyone on track and on message.

I've found that using a simple email invitation, an e-vitation, is the most effective method of getting people on board. All the links and communication information need to be embedded in the e-vite, and it must be self-explanatory. Dry runs by the presenters on all of the technology and presentation material are mandatory.

Webinars can be a powerful tool for communicating with a broad audience. If you have a compelling topic and a recognized, articulate, and respected co presenter who is a client, I'd encourage you to use this medium to maximum effectiveness.

Story Time:

This is a short one. We had developed a new service offering and had done a targeted, initial visibility campaign and spent considerable time and effort putting together marketing materials. We wanted to see what the response would be in the broader market for the service so we put together an e-vite and sent it out to approximately 500 prospects and existing clients. We had 95+ connect to the Webinar and they stayed for the whole hour. Subsequently we were able to meet with a number of them and secure new contracts. Our total investment in time for the Webinar was miniscule compared to how long it would have taken to get this information out into the marketplace the old fashioned way.

William C. Johnson

Bite #22
Be a Coach

As you grow professionally and learn new skills one of the ways you can make yourself even more valuable to your firm is if you consciously "pass it forward". Take your learning and teach others.

Take them by the hand, sometimes literally, and show them how true, relational business development is done. Make the time to mentor the ones who express a desire to learn these tremendously important and valuable skills.

This can be done in a formal way through a series of lunch time sessions or you can make a practice of taking some of the likely candidates with you on calls to see what you do, experience what a real profession interview feels like, expand their horizons beyond the office walls and know what it's like to learn something new about someone new.

Coaching others is probably one of the quickest ways to cement the learnings of this book into your own mind so I would encourage you to do this. Make this piece of your professional business development mosaic as you put the pieces together, help someone else complete theirs.

William C. Johnson

Bite #23
Golf

Where do I even begin on this one? If you don't play, consider starting. If you do start, play at least 18 holes every week for two seasons just to get semi-proficient. It really takes time, and you'll develop a deep appreciation for the men and women of the PGA and LPGA and what they do weekly, for it is truly amazing.

If you do play and you play poorly, which all of us do at the beginning and at random other times for any one of about a thousand reasons, at least play fast. Bad golf is slow golf. No one will say a thing if you stink up the course, but do it at a fast pace.

Now, why golf? It is by far one of the quickest ways to cement lasting relationships with people and maintain them. There is just something about spending five hours talking about nothing other than how lousy the greens are, why those losers in front of us can't get it together and stop looking for lost balls in the pucker brush….it's magical.

I can trace any number of major relationships that led to major projects back to a strategic game of golf with either a team member or a client. It just works. If you know someone who plays reasonably well, ask them to help you. We all started in the same place, we all were horrible, and no one ever forgets, so there's plenty of empathy on a golf course.

So go ahead and get started. I won't start to tell golf stories; there are too many and I could write an entire book on the people that I've met and the projects I've won without saying a word about them on the golf course. And remember: don't talk shop on the course; that's for lunch or dinner and a beer afterwards. Invariably within two weeks the phone will ring and your golf partner will say something like, "didn't you mention that your firm did blahblahblah? Do you think you could come in and meet with a couple of people to talk about that?" It has happened more times than I can count.

Business Development for Professionals

Bite #24
Closing Philosophy

William C. Johnson

I could go on and discuss all sorts of incidentals, but you know all about them, and if you don't, you'll learn by doing what we've already discussed. Look sharp, dress professionally, mind you manners, don't chew gum or smoke, and watch your language....I sound like your mother!

I would like to close with a thought that I spoke about earlier that I want to reiterate, it's that important. Some people will look at your success over the years and try to attribute it to a lot of things or combination of them, but there is one major component that is the most important. This is the maxim under which I operate: "It's all about helping."

If you attend all the organizational meetings, get on the committees, write the articles for trade publications, do webinars, contact ten people every week just to chat and ten more for lead generation, get out to client and team member meetings and events and do this with the goal of helping all who you meet, you will be successful.

People may not remember exactly where they've seen you, but they just know that they have, and if you are motivated by helping others, there is a good chance that they are going to remember it when they need something. This attitude will reap great relational rewards and the business will follow.

Also, remember that there is no luck in business development; you make your own – by persevering, by being out there, by helping more people than anyone you know and by showing up. To reiterate "If you appear to be everywhere all of the time you are bound to be in the right place some of the time."

Story Time:

A senior facility manager at very small private secondary school called about engineering services and said that they got our name from one of our largest existing clients who was very familiar with us.

I needed a break from the office and also wanted to meet whatever expectations our existing client contact might have so I made an appointment with the school and went to the meeting. It was pretty much as I expected.

Their planning process was a shambles and they really didn't need engineering support what they needed was a whole planning and group interaction support process to help with strategic planning. I left with the task of putting together a brief letter detailing what we'd put together for a scope at the meeting for the board of directors to mull over. This letter was actually going to land on the desk of our client contact who, come to find out, was sitting on their board of directors, and it gets even more interesting.

I went back to the office and shared this information about this meeting with a co-worker in passing and she immediately recognized the existing clients name as being the prime contact for a rather large series of significant projects. You just never know where things are going to lead, so you need to always be paying attention and making those connections. So now we had the opportunity to help this client's alma mater and at the same time expose him to a planning process model that we've been thinking might work for them. All of this activity flowed from just showing up at what I thought would be a rather small project with a very small school.

These are the stories that I keep in the back of my mind when I am considering whether to show up or not, and these are the stories that motivate me to keep showing up where I can't see any immediate, short-term benefit. If these were random occurrences, I'd be skeptical, but they're not; these things happen all the time, motivating me to just keep showing up.

Closing Thoughts:

Thank you for the time that you've taken to read this very short, simple book on business development. I hope that I've given you some things to think about and do. The learning is in the "doing," so go and do!

I also wanted to share that I've been blessed and count myself so. I've been blessed with a wife and my two grown girls who have always been supportive and a network of family, close friends and business friends who are second to none, and it has developed in me a heart full of gratitude.

Not a day goes by that I don't thank God for how I've been blessed and taken care of. My hope for you is that God will bless you in your quest to be the best help to the people around you that have been given into your care.

CPSIA information can be obtained at www.ICGtesting.com
Printed in the USA
BVOW02s0609201114

375866BV00001B/8/P